# Beyond this World
# Science Fiction

## by David Orme

# Contents

Longman

Edinburgh Gate
Harlow, Essex

*'Ally and the Forty Monsters' is based on the story of Ali Baba and the forty thieves from* The Arabian Nights. *In that story, Ali Baba overhears the secret password of the thieves' treasure cave.*

# Ally and the Forty Monsters

**1**

Kevin's friend Ally had a sister called Sarah, and Sarah was the meanest person he knew!

Sarah had a computer game called 'Invasion of the Forty Monsters'. It was a virtual reality game. You put on a helmet that covered your eyes and ears. You felt as if you were really there. It was the best game ever – but she wouldn't let anyone else have a go!

"I paid for it, so I'm keeping it for myself," she said.

Ally and Kevin begged, but Sarah wouldn't change her mind. "Buy your own," she said. Kevin and Ally couldn't. They were broke! They had to play with their old games.

One day Kevin was in Ally's room. Sarah was in her room playing the game.

"Let's sneak in when she's not there and try it," said Kevin.

"That's no good. You have to say a password to start the game, and another one to end it."

Just then Sarah came out.

"Still playing that old game?" she said. "You two need to get up to date!"

"Come on, let us have a go!"

Sarah laughed. "No chance!" she said.

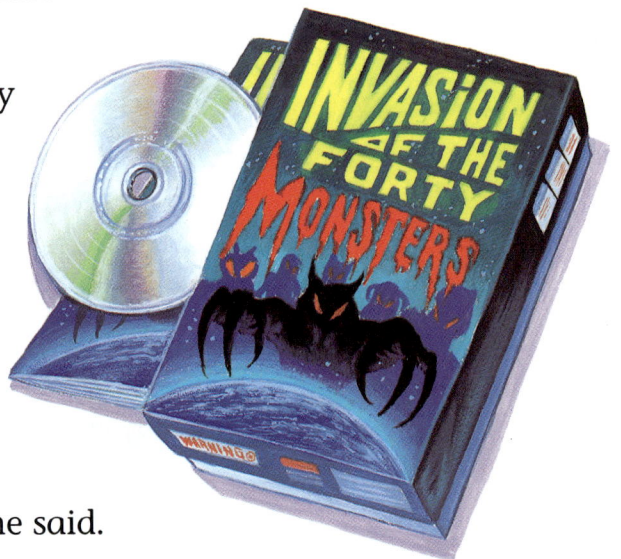

## 2

It was suppertime. Ally's Dad was annoyed. He had called Sarah, but she couldn't hear anything when she wore the special helmet.

"Ally, go and fetch your sister." said Mr Barber. "Tell her the dog is about to get her supper."

Ally went up and banged on Sarah's door. She still couldn't hear. Ally went in. He heard his sister say "Rats!"

Sarah was angry.

"Who said you could come into my room?"

"Dad sent me. The dog is about to get your supper."

"We haven't got a dog."

"That's true. I'll have it then."

Grumbling, Sarah came downstairs. Ally was excited. He knew one of Sarah's passwords. He couldn't wait to tell Kevin!

## 3

Next day Kevin was back at Ally's.

"I know one of the passwords. Rats! She said it when I went in!"

"That's no good. It's the password to end the program. We need the one that starts it."

Ally hadn't thought of that!

"Wait!" said Kevin. "I've got an idea! 'Rats' ends the game. Maybe to start it you have to say 'rats' backwards."

Ally's eyes lit up. They had both passwords. Sarah was going out that evening. That would be his chance!

**4**

Ally put the helmet on and said the password. Suddenly he was high up on a rocky ledge. Mountains covered with snow stretched into the distance. Far below was a forest with a great river winding through it like a blue snake.

It felt as if he was really there. He could even move around just by thinking about it. Nearby was the edge of a cliff. It was only a game, but Ally stayed away from there. He didn't like heights!

Just then he heard a stamping and roaring. The forty monsters were coming!

**5**

They jumped out from behind the rocks and marched towards Ally. They all had sharp claws, and big teeth sticking out of slimy mouths.

Ally was terrified. He knew he had to fight them, but he hadn't read the instructions! Nearer and nearer the monsters came. Ally kept backing away. Suddenly he fell backwards over the cliff!

The feeling of falling was horrible. Ally desperately tried to remember the password to finish the game. He had forgotten it! The ground got nearer and nearer.

Then he heard a voice.

"Rats!" it said.

Ally was back in Sarah's room. He thought Sarah would be angry but she was laughing at him.

"You've turned green and your hair is standing on end!" she said.

Ally groaned. "I'll read the instructions next time!" he said.

"No, you won't!" said Sarah. "Clear off. I'm going to change the password!"

*Note: Did you work out the secret password that started the game?*

*'Holiday Rock' is based on the legend of King Arthur, the 'Once and Future King' who pulled a sword from a rock, not knowing that this was the test for who was to be the King.*

# Holiday Rock

**1**

"We've got problems!"

"What's up, Dad?" said Arthur.

"Not sure. Merlin's about to report."

"Spacecraft damaged by collision with dust cloud. Land immediately and wait for help," said the computer.

Mum groaned.

"First day of the holiday and this has to happen. I knew a space tour was a bad idea!"

Dad ignored this. "Merlin, where is the nearest safe landing?"

"Four light years from here is an Earth-type planet, category 5B."

"What's a 5B?" asked Arthur.

Dad knew.

"It's a planet with intelligent beings on it. They are still at an early stage of development, so they are meant to be left alone. No landing except in an emergency."

"Well, this is an emergency!"

"Right. Merlin, set a course!"

## 2

From space, the planet looked just like Earth – blue seas, green forests, and brown areas of desert. Carefully, the Merlin guided the damaged spacecraft in.

They landed in a green valley. All looked peaceful. Too peaceful, thought Mum.

"How long have we got to wait?"

"It won't be long. The computer called the Astronaut's Association as soon as the accident happened. They will be here in three days."

"Three days!"

Arthur knew a row was about to start. He slipped quietly out of the ship.

They had landed near a forest. Arthur wandered through the trees. It was very beautiful. The trees were like many-coloured ferns, and brightly coloured birds chattered among the fronds. In sunny clearings, gold and silver insects hovered over enormous flowers.

In the centre of one of the clearings Arthur found a mossy rock. Something was shining there. It was a sword, half-buried in the rock.

It was a beautiful sword, and Arthur wanted it.

**3**

He tugged and tugged, but the sword wouldn't budge. "No problem!" thought Arthur. He chose a tool from his backpack and pointed it at the rock. Slowly, the rock around the sword turned to dust. He gave it another tug, and it was free.

"Great!" thought Arthur. He put the tool back in his bag and, holding the sword carefully, turned to go.

It was then that he found out that he wasn't alone.

The natives of the planet looked quite human, though they wore simple clothes. They carried spears. Arthur didn't like the look of them. He knew he had to get back to the ship quickly – but he wasn't going to give up his sword! He set off through the forest as fast as he could go.

Arthur's parents were surprised when he came running in, chased by spear-carrying tribespeople. Dad shut the door quickly.

"You idiot! You know you are not meant to make contact!"

They looked outside. They expected to see angry people waving spears about. What they didn't expect was to see them laughing and dancing, and throwing flowers at the ship!

"I think they like me!" said Arthur. He told his parents about finding the sword. They were extremely cross.

"Merlin," said Dad. "What do you suggest?"

"The sword must be returned," said Merlin. That was all the computer would say.

Arthur felt very nervous walking back to the forest surrounded by cheering crowds. They kept bowing to him. When he got back to the rock he pushed the sword back in and sealed it with a different tool. No-one would shift that in a hurry!

One by one the bravest of the tribespeople tried to pull the sword out of the stone, but it was stuck fast. They turned to Arthur to see him do it again – but Arthur had slipped away, back to the ship.

The tribespeople didn't mind. The King had come – one day, he would come again.

*'The Last Invasion' uses the story of Odysseus and his adventure with Polyphemus, a one-eyed giant, or Cyclops. You will find the original story in* The Odyssey *by the Greek poet Homer.*

# The Last Invasion

**1**

"Keep alert, team."

Mike was captain of the spaceship *Calypso*. He led a team that explored unknown planets. They had landed the ship near a deserted city.

"This empty city is weird," said Kate, Mike's second-in-command. "I wonder where the people who built it have gone?"

"Maybe it was a war," said Jon, the team's scientist.

The team reached a huge white building. It had once had wooden doors, but they had rotted away.

"I'd like to go in there," said Jon. "We might be able to learn something about the people who lived here."

Cautiously, the three explorers went in. They found themselves in a grand hall. The room contained a few odd-looking metal chairs. On one wall there was an enormous picture. It looked like a battle scene. Human-looking creatures were fighting what looked like lizard men.

"It looks like an alien invasion," said Mike. "They must have been fighting them for a long time if they were able to paint this picture."

"But if the aliens won, where are they?" said Kate.

Just then, they heard a sound behind them. Someone – or something – had followed them into the building!

## 2

An enormous robot was standing in the doorway. It looked green and scaly, like the lizard men in the picture, but it only had one eye.

"It doesn't look very friendly," whispered Kate.

The robot was completely blocking the door. There was another door near the picture. Jon tried to open it, but it was made of hard metal and would not open.

Mike decided to see if the robot was friendly. He walked cautiously towards it. The robot watched him with its one eye and pointed an arm at him. A blue flash came from the robot's hand. Mike jumped back.

"Ow, that hurt!" he said. "He doesn't want us to leave!"

The robot didn't hurt the explorers again. It just stood in the doorway. They were trapped!

"Any ideas, Jon?" said Mike.

"It must be programmed to keep us prisoner. Perhaps it is waiting for the lizard creatures to arrive."

"But there aren't any!"

"Yes, but it doesn't know that. We could be here for a long time!"

# 3

It was boring sitting in the huge room. Kate switched on her personal music centre. "Let's listen to some music," she said.

The beat of the music filled the room, and the robot started to move!

"Hey, it looks as if he likes it!" said Mike.

The robot was behaving very strangely. He did a clumsy dance round the room, then fell over, then got up again. At last he lay on his back on the floor, his metal legs waving in the air.

"I didn't think the music was that bad!" said Kate.

"It's the beat!" said Jon. "It's affecting his circuits!"

"I've got a plan!" said Mike. "Kate, keep playing the music. He can't walk, but he can still see you. Dance around a bit, keep him occupied."

Using all his strength, Mike broke off a length of metal from one of the chairs. While Kate and Jon danced, he crept round behind the robot. Suddenly, he smashed down at the robot's eye with his metal bar.

"Come on! He can't see us now!"

They rushed out and hurried back to the spaceship, keeping a watch for any more robots.

Later, Mike was writing his report. "I suppose the lizard men wiped out the humans, then died of some disease," he said.

Jon shook his head. "Those chairs were designed for lizard people. It was the human types who were the invaders. The robot was defending his planet."

The team looked at each other. They all felt guilty now.

"To him, we were the invaders," said Jon.

'The Robot Builder's Apprentice' is based on the story of 'The Sorcerer's Apprentice'. This story is told in a poem called 'Der Zauberlehrling' by the German poet Goethe. In the poem the apprentice finds the Sorcerer's book of spells and makes the broom bring in water. He can't find the spell to make it stop! Zauber means sorcerer or magician, so I used this as a name in the story.

There is a famous piece of music based on the story of 'The Sorcerer's Apprentice' by the French composer Paul Dukas. The music was used in the Walt Disney film 'Fantasia', with Mickey Mouse as the apprentice.

# The Robot Builder's Apprentice

"And while I'm out, clean up this laboratory!"

Tara groaned. She had been excited when she came to work for the world's greatest expert in robots. She had always hoped that, one day, she would be able to design and build robots herself. All she had done so far was tidy up. It seemed she couldn't even get that right. Professor Zauber was short tempered and grumpy, and always found fault.

She looked around. Bits and pieces lay all over the place. Work on electronics should be done in dust-free places, but it seemed that Professor Zauber didn't care about that – there was dust everywhere.

Tara started on the professor's main workbench. Next to it stood an impressive-looking robot. The professor was designing it for a company that made cleaning equipment. It was programmed to do every sort of cleaning – dusting, tidying – even washing up. It was called 'Magic Broom Mark 23' and was very nearly finished. The battery lay on the bench, ready to be plugged in.

It was then that Tara got her idea.

"I'm fed up with slaving away," she thought. "I'll let Magic Broom take the strain!"

She clipped in the batteries. Magic Broom's eyes glowed.

"I am your cleaning robot for today. How may I help you?"

"Get this place cleaned up!"

Magic Broom's eyes swept round the room. Its super-sensitive nose came out on a stalk and waved around in the air. Dust!

The robot opened its chest and took out a brush. It swept the dust into a heap, then a mini-vacuum cleaner in its finger sucked it up. It certainly knew its job: it picked up equipment, dusted underneath, then carefully put it back.

Magic Broom moved onto the bench where the professor worked with chemicals. It was covered with dirty beakers and test tubes. The robot went to the sink and pushed in the plug. It then turned on both taps. Water gushed out, spraying out over the laboratory.

"Hey, turn the water down a bit!" said Tara.

Magic Broom took no notice. The robot started to fill the sink with washing up. Soon the sink was full, and the water started running down onto the floor.

Tara tried to turn the taps off but Magic Broom had jammed them on. They were stuck! She tried to take the glassware out of the sink, but Magic Broom just kept putting it back.

"Hey, you stupid machine, just stop, will you!" Tara yelled.

Magic Broom stopped.

"I am your cleaning robot for today. How may I help you?"

"Don't do anything!"

Magic Broom thought about this.

"Task not completed!" it said. It started filling the sink again.

Water had now reached the door.

"If this is Mark 23, I wonder what all the others were like!" thought Tara.

Then she had an idea. The batteries! She tried to open the battery cover. Magic Broom firmly removed her hand.

"Task not completed!" it said again.

More and more water poured over the floor. Tara was in despair. What would Professor Zauber say? She would be sacked for sure!

The laboratory door burst open. Horrified, Professor Zauber looked at the chaos in his laboratory. He turned the water off at the mains supply then marched over to the robot and hit a red switch that Tara hadn't noticed on its shoulder.

"Have a nice day!" said Magic Broom – then it stopped.

Professor Zauber looked at the laboratory, and at the robot, and at Tara. Then he started to laugh. He laughed so much that he had to sit down.

When he finished laughing, he started working at his bench.

"What are you doing?" said Tara nervously.

"I'm getting started on Mark 24, of course!"

*'Mr Dutch' is based on the legend of the Flying Dutchman. In the legend the Dutchman is the victim of a curse; he has to sail the seas forever.*

# Mr Dutch

**1**

Karen and Michael liked their neighbour. Mr Dutch chatted to them for hours. He knew an amazing amount about every period of history. Whatever the twins were studying Mr Dutch could bring to life with stories about characters from the past. Sometimes this had got the twins into trouble with their history teacher.

"You must only write what you know to be true," she said. "Look at what you've written here: 'Julius Caesar always sang in the baths, which drove everyone mad because he couldn't sing!' Now how could you possibly know that? You mustn't just make things up, you know!"

But Mr Dutch had told them and the twins were sure it was true. His stories were so good it was almost as if he had been there.

## 2

One day a 'For Sale' board went up next door. The twins were upset.

"It's time for me to move on," said Mr Dutch that evening. I never stay for more than five years in any one place."

"Why?"

"I'm just a wanderer. I always have been."

The twins asked him to give them his new address.

"I'm not sure where I am going yet. I'll send you a postcard as soon as I am settled."

And that was all he would say.

The day came when Mr Dutch moved out. He had sold his furniture with the house. He just had a few suitcases and boxes which he packed into his car.

He came round to say goodbye to the twins, and to ask their parents a favour.

"Your new neighbours won't be moving in yet. Could you keep an eye on the house while it is empty? I'll leave you a key."

Mr Dutch waved goodbye and drove off. Karen and Michael didn't think they would ever see him again.

## 3

A few days later the twins' father went across to check the house. Karen and Michael went too. The furniture was still in its place, but the cupboards were empty – except one. In the back of a wardrobe Michael found a big scrapbook, full of old photographs and newspaper cuttings.

"I'm sure he didn't mean to leave this," said Dad. "We'll take it home and look after it. When he gets in touch we'll send it on."

That evening Michael came down and borrowed the scrapbook. He called Karen in and they started looking through it. The newspaper cuttings were old and in foreign languages – not very interesting.

The photographs were old, too. One of them showed an ancient railway engine with people standing around it. There was a date written underneath it – 1872. Karen looked closely at the faded picture, and gasped.

"It's Mr Dutch!"

He was in Victorian clothes, with a tall 'stove-pipe' hat, but it was unmistakably Mr Dutch.

**4**

Two days later a car pulled up beside the twins. They felt
alarmed, but it wasn't a stranger. It was Mr Dutch.

"I've just been back to the house," he said. "I left something
behind, but I can't find it."

"Was it a scrapbook?"

"Yes. Have you looked in it?"

The children nodded guiltily.

Mr Dutch got out of the car. The park was nearby. He sat down
on a bench with the twins.

"I've never told anyone this before, but I expect you've guessed,"
he said.

Karen nodded. "I think I know. You come from the past, don't you?"

Mr Dutch shook his head. "No, I come from the future."

## 5

"I was, or rather I will be – born in 2409," he said. "I built time machines. I could go anywhen."

"Anywhen?"

"It's like anywhere, only in time, not space! I went back to Rome. I even met Julius Caesar!"

"Did he really sing badly?" asked Karen.

"It was terrible! Anyway, my time machine was damaged. I became trapped in the past."

"Hang on!" said Michael. "That was two thousand years ago! How can you still be alive?"

"I can't begin to age again until I reach my own time – that's what happens when you travel in time. I have been the same age for over 2,000 years. In four hundred years I will reach my proper time – only then can I grow old."

Mr Dutch called round that evening and collected the scrapbook. The twins kept his secret – all their lives. They never saw him again, but they knew that, somewhere in the world, he was wandering, waiting patiently – for the present.

*The idea for 'The Lord of the Universe' came from the play* Macbeth *by William Shakespeare. In the play three witches reveal Macbeth's future. Their predictions come true, but not in the way Macbeth expects!*

# The Lord of the Galaxy

*In the darkness of interstellar space, far from any civilised world, lay the Dead Zone. Millions of years ago, a mighty space war had been fought here; now nothing was left but the dry cinders of long-dead planets orbiting shrunken stars.*

*On one planet, however, there was life – of a sort. Not life that lived and breathed, but the cold, ageless intelligence of computers …*

**1**

Spaceship *Dunsinane* was lost. Returning from a battle with the alien empire, the navigating systems had gone down.

"I'm getting a signal," said Lieutenant Banks. "But it's not from the fleet. It's coming from that dead planet ahead."

Captain Mack was amazed.

"Nothing has lived on that planet for millions of years!" he said.

"It seems to be coming from a computer below the surface."

Suddenly the lights on the bridge went out. A red glow appeared in the middle of the room. A cold, mechanical voice started speaking.

"Greetings, Captain Mack."

"Who are you? How do you know my name?"

A second voice spoke.

"We know everything that is, and everything that will be, Captain Mack – Ruler of Planet Cawdor!"

"But I'm not Ruler of Planet Cawdor, I'm just …"

A third voice interrupted him.

"Captain Mack, who will be Lord of the Galaxy!"

Suddenly, the voices disappeared. The light came on. Another voice spoke, but this time on ship-to-ship radio.

"Spaceship *Ross* calling *Dunsinane*. Are you lost? Take a bearing and we'll lead you home! Oh, and by the way, we've got a message for Captain Mack. Now the war is over you've got a new job – Ruler of Planet Cawdor! Congratulations!"

## 2

Mack's wife was delighted with her husband's new job. She now lived in a palace on planet Cawdor with androids to do all of the work. Androids were robots, but they looked just like human beings.

She couldn't help remembering the coded message Captain Mack had sent her from space:

'They said I would rule Cawdor, and they got that right. Then they said I would be Lord of the Galaxy …'

It so happened that Duncan, President of the Grand Council of the Galaxy, was coming to Cawdor to visit his old friend Mack.

"If Duncan died, they would make you President in his place!" Mack's wife whispered. "You must kill him!"

"But what if we were found out?"

"Then we will suffer. But it's worth taking the chance!"

At last Mack agreed to kill Duncan. Secretly, he took off from the planet. If he could destroy Duncan's ship in deep space, no-one would ever know what happened to it.

Mack lay in wait for the ship, hidden in the dust of a nebula. At last his scanners picked it up. Duncan's ship, with the newly promoted Captain Banks in charge – the only other person who knew about the computers on the dark planet!

Mack fired his laser cannon at the defenceless ship.

## 3

In his state apartments President Mack was enjoying a drink when a computer pinged. A message! A face looked at him from the screen.

It was Captain Banks!

"Mack, I know it is you attacking this ship, " said Banks. "I know the ship is doomed and I will be dead when you get this message, but don't think you can get away with it. In some way I will reach out from my grave in space … and destroy you!"

The message ended. Mack was shaking. His face had turned grey.

"He's got some plan to destroy me, I know it!" he thought. "I must go back to the Dead Zone. Those computers know everything – the past, the present and future. They will tell me what I must do!"

## 4

Once more, Mack's ship floated in the Dead Zone. Once more, the computers spoke.

"What do you wish to learn?"
"What is going to happen to me? Will I be killed?"

The second voice spoke.
"No man can kill you, President Mack."

Mack was relieved. As he returned home, he laughed at his fears.

Half-way back, a signal came from another ship. A face appeared on the ship-to-ship screen.

"My name is Duff. Captain Banks sent me to kill you."
"No man can kill me!" sneered Mack. "The computer said so!"
Duff smiled. "But I'm not a man. I'm an android."

He hit a button and Mack's ship exploded into a million stars.